Route 80A: Morden to Walton-on-the-Hill, via Sutton, 31st December 1974.

Colin Sackett

Printed landscape

Uniformbooks 2019

First published 2019
Copyright © Colin Sackett
Frontispiece photo by David Jones
ISBN 978–1–910010–19–8

Uniformbooks
7 Hillhead Terrace, Axminster, Devon EX13 5JL
www.uniformbooks.co.uk

Trade distribution in the UK by Central Books
www.centralbooks.com

Printed and bound by T J International, Padstow, Cornwall

"No ideas but in ink…"

....

"...the practically cognized present is no knife edge, but a saddle-back, with a certain breadth of its own on which we sit perched, and from which we look in two directions into time. The unit of composition of our perception of time is a *duration*, with a bow and a stern, as it were—a rearward- and a forward-looking end. It is only as parts of this *duration-block* that the relation of *succession* of one end to the other is perceived. We do not first feel one end and then feel the other after it, and from the perception of the succession infer an interval of time between, but we seem to feel the interval of time as a whole, with its two ends embedded in it."
—William James *The Principles of Psychology*, 1890.

"A river is a line of water not a narrative."—Anon.

Typewritten terms and abbreviations from the map of a suburban area measuring ten by ten kilometres: 'TQ26, Ordnance Survey 1:25000 second series'. Each kilometre square is superimposed; the accumulative interference isolating each locational term from relationships within its own territory. Index, p.10.

Aggregate

This geography—a hundred square kilometres that are part of the London Boroughs of Sutton, Merton and Croydon—is the area where I spent my childhood. It includes the schools and parks and libraries that I went to, and the type of place with which I was most familiar during my first twenty years.

Ten or fifteen years later, in the early 1990s and living in central London, I would travel out to this area and walk from one familiar place to another. There seemed to me to be specific ideas of connectedness, a psychological understanding of the way locations are related to each other. Places are linked by roads and people mainly travel from here to there by car, or bus, the bits in-between largely filled with houses and gardens, all making a particular mental geography of the suburbs. This can perhaps be best understood in contrast to another *isolative* perceptual geography: that of a single feature related to its particular topography, for example, a hill farm in a rural landscape.

One part of this suburban landscape seemed anomalous, its 'identity' could be perceived as an 'inverted wilderness': a large flat area bordering Mitcham, Carshalton, Croydon and Wallington—a square mile or so—of officially private rough land, gravel pits and ex-sewage workings. There is a network of paths and the whole area is fenced-off (unofficial access is available about every few hundred yards). The area is used for riding motorbikes, rabbiting, watching birds, etc.; marginal activities.

Bounded on all sides by arterial roads and a railway line, from within the fenced-off area there is a feeling of detachment and in effect, *invisibility*. From a car one is aware of the perimeter and the power lines that cross the area, and five miles away, on the horizon, you can see the buildings of central Croydon. It seems to correspond to the opposite of the land beyond the medieval town walls—this perimeter containing the town and keeping out the land, whereas here the 'wild' is an island within the suburban.

Some hypothetical ideas of orientation in landscape were provoked by being here—that there may exist a sort of historical and acoustical 'depth' in the place, a pre-electrical *radio* of invisible/inaudible sound.

Allot Gdns: Allotment Gardens
BP: Boundary Post or Plate
BS: Boundary Stone
Cemy: Cemetery
CH: Club House
Coll: College
Ct: Court
F Sta: Fire Station
FB: Foot Bridge
Hospl: Hospital
Liby: Library
MS: Mile Stone

PO: Post Office
Pol Sta: Police Station
Recn Gd: Recreation Ground
Resr: Reservoir
Sch: School
Spr: Spring
Sta: Station
TA: Territorial Army
TH: Town Hall
W: Well
War Meml: War Memorial
Wks: Works

Bbbn

engraved circular scenes cut into empty boxwood
bobbins that may print some continual landscape

Collection

....

"The traditional bunch consists of a collection of watercress stems, about 140mm in length weighing about 110g and held together by a rubber band. The brand name, address and Code of Practice number of the producer should be included on a small rectangular card inserted in the bunch."

—Watercress, production of the cultivated crop, London 1983.

In the early 1980s I began to save the card labels that commonly came with bunches of watercress. As well as the grower's name and location, the roughly uniform strips would often state the watery conditions of 'purity', and 'coolness', necessary for commercial production and distribution. Each label—Kingfisher, Lustrecress, Sylvasprings—tethered the cress to a typical and identifiable landscape: a clay and chalk valley with water from a spring, or raised from boreholes, channelled to flow gently across wide beds of screeded concrete and gravel. Seen from above, these planned rectilinear forms impose upon and contrast with the undulating topography on the ground.

But some time recently such labels have disappeared, along with the rubber band, as the packaging of watercress has changed almost entirely to sealed plastic bags, chilled and loose, and kept fresh at fridge temperature. As with much cultivation, larger sites have been developed and many smaller farms have given up or been absorbed, the number of growers declining in response to the exacting demands of the centralised market. It became clear that there was finality to this collection of ephemera, as examples dwindled from occasional to almost none. No longer is it possible to identify and connect similarity and likeness; the diversity of layouts and colours—these printed landscapes—are now gathered and fixed to the activity and geography of their time.

p.13–22: Actual size illustrations.

LONGCOMBE WATERCRESS
Organically Cultivated Watercress
Lower Longcombe Farm, TOTNES 863259

Red ink

SPREADEAGLE WATERCRESS
GROWN IN SPRING WATER — WILLIAMSON, LUDWELL, WILTS

Blue ink

HURD'S SPRING VALLEY
WATERCRESS
CULTIVATED BY J. H. W. HURD
HILL DEVERILL, WARMINSTER.

Blue ink

Chalke Valley

Blue ink

SELECTED BUNCHED WATERCRESS
GROWN IN THE CHALK SPRINGS OF
THE TEST VALLEY, HAMPSHIRE
By L. C. BIGGS, WHITCHURCH, HAMPSHIRE

Red ink

'Kingfisher'
SUPREME WATERCRESS

Blue ink / Red ink

CODE OF PRACTICE REGISTERED
No. 168

Blue ink

'*Kingfisher*' watercress is grown in sparkling spring water drawn from beneath the Surrey Hills and packed under most hygienic conditions by R. COE & Sons, Abinger Hammer, DORKING.

Blue ink / Red ink

GREEN STAR
WATERCRESS
GROWN IN PURE SPRING WATER
TO N.F.U. CODE OF PRACTICE STANDARDS
CRICKLADE NURSERIES, ANDOVER, HANTS. TEL. 2475

Green ink

 DOUBLE DIAMOND
WATERCRESS
GROWN IN PURE SPRING WATER
TO N.F.U. CODE OF PRACTICE STANDARDS
CRICKLADE NURSERIES, ANDOVER, HANTS.

Red ink

Blue ink

SELECTED BUNCHED WATERCRESS

By L. C. BIGGS, WHITCHURCH, HANTS

Red ink

★ ★ **BIGOS** ★ ★
★ **WATERCRESS**

Green ink

 **HOLWELL WATERCRESS**
CRANBORNE   Tel. 0725 517301
DORSET
ALWAYS WASH BEFORE USE

YOUR
ASSURANCE OF
HYGENIC
PRODUCTION
REGISTERED NO.114

Blue ink

 SEND 3 OF THESE TICKETS,
PLUS (SAE 9" x 6")
FOR A FREE WATERCRESS
RECIPE BOOK

Red ink

CULTIVATED IN SPRING WATER

BY A. W. & R. W. BIGGS, WHITCHURCH, HANTS.

Green ink

WATCH FOR
HAIR SPRING
WATERCRESS

Green ink

HAIRSPRING WATERCRESS
CODE OF PRACTICE REG. NO. 167
WASH BEFORE USE

Green ink

RED LABEL

Red ink

Sylvasprings   Waddock X
Dorchester, Dorset

Blue ink

WESSEX WATERCRESS   Waddock X
Dorchester, Dorset

Black ink

LUSTRECRESS   Dorchester · Dorset

Blue ink

TRADITIONAL ENGLISH WATERCRESS GROWN
FOR OVER 100 YEARS IN PUREST SPRING WATER
FROM THE SUSSEX DOWNS BY
HAIRSPRING WATERCRESS

Green ink

WATERCRESS GROWN BY:- **KEEP**
A.W. & R.W. BIGGS, **COOL**
WHITCHURCH, HAMPSHIRE. **AND**
MOIST

Red ink

Produced according to Approved Watercress Code of
Practice—Registered No. 123

Blue ink

Produced according to Approved Watercress Code of
Practice—Registered No. 123

Black ink

Green ink / Magenta ink

Ochre ink

Blue ink

Blue ink

Green ink / Blue ink

Green ink

FREE WATERCRESS RECIPE BOOK
SEND 9" x 6½" S.A.E. TO
ADDRESS OVER OTHER SIDE
WASH BEFORE USE

UKROFS
ORGANIC
11UKF060162

Green ink / Magenta ink

WATERCRESS
PACKED BY B. & M. WATERCRESS LTD.
FOR FREE RECIPE BOOK SEND LARGE 9 x 6 S.A.E. TO THE
ABOVE AT THE NYTHE, ALRESFORD, HANTS. SO24 9DZ.

Ochre ink

SUPERCRESS

From Alresford, Hampshire—Code of Practice Registered No. 199

Blue ink

Grown to the N.F.U. Watercress Association
Code of Practice Standards
by **J. T. & J. H. MILLS**, Alresford, Hampshire
Registered No. 199

Blue ink

CULTIVATED IN PURE SPRING WATER
By **J.T. & J.H. MILLS** ALRESFORD HAMPSHIRE
GROWN TO N.F.U. WATERCRESS BRANCH
CODE OF PRACTICE REGISTERED No.199

Green ink

WATERCRESS
PACKED BY THE WATERCRESS COMPANY LTD
THOROUGHLY WASH BEFORE USE
KEEP IN REFRIGERATOR

Green ink

Black ink

Green ink

Blue ink

Blue ink

Green ink

Blue ink

WASH THOROUGHLY BEFORE USE. To store, wash, shake off surplus water and refrigerate in airtight container. For our colour recipe and code of practice fact booklet send large SAE to Vitacress Salads Ltd., Fobdown, Alresford, Hampshire, SO24 9TD.

Green ink

CULTIVATED IN SPRING WATER

BY A. W. & R. W. BIGGS, WHITCHURCH, HANTS.

Blue ink

GROWN TO N.F.U. WATERCRESS BRANCH CODE OF PRACTICE

WATERCRESS GROWN BY:-
A.W. & R.W. BIGGS.
WHITCHURCH, HAMPSHIRE.
CODE OF PRACTICE REG. No. 190

KEEP
COOL
AND
MOIST

Blue ink

HAMPSHIRE WATERCRESS LIMITED
FOBDOWN   ALRESFORD   HAMPSHIRE

Green ink

WASH THOROUGHLY BEFORE USE. To store, wash, shake off surplus water and refrigerate in airtight container. For our colour recipe and code of practice fact booklet send large SAE to Sylvasprings Watercress Ltd., Vitacress House, New Farm Road, Alresford, Hants. SO24 9QH.

Blue ink

Directory

A cluster of buildings, a house and office, various working and storage units: milking parlours, shelters, barns, etc.

p.24–25: Local 'Farmers', annotated *Yellow Pages*, 1998. p.26–29: Aerial views and phone numbers. [p.30–31]: Locational phone numbers.

25

32238

32242

32305

32314

32320

32326

32359

32389

881493

881356

881386   881367   881304

881258   881203
                              32344

831250   33263
  831270   32389
                                        33267

                              32347
        33310

    32320
        32368   33093   3230
831225   33496   33074

831346   33867
                  32294

              33193   32314
33194   32238
        552235
552587   33541
        552229
552237
                              33283
        552865
552205   552614

                        552556

        553379
    553290   553047
553928   552244   553462
                  552544
                                    3336
552261

        552523
                      552371

678234

678208

678327

678304

33330   33125   678261   678246

32179   678293

32887   678295

678341   678268

33067   678271

2242   678287   678252

32395

32022

33322   32962   678321

33782

33329 32305   34525

765   33323

32148

33483   32343

26   560600

32402   560479

560428

442994

32131

443057

Escarpment

p.33–36: 'Land Forms' *Intermediate Map Reading*, Thomas Pickles, London 1949.

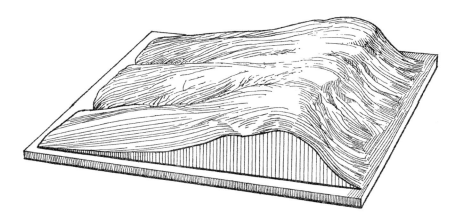

printed line

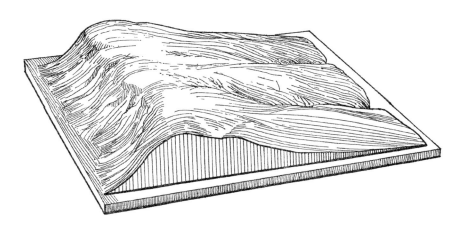

of a section

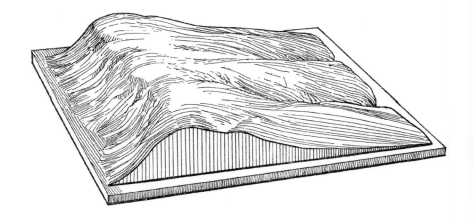

drawing of a

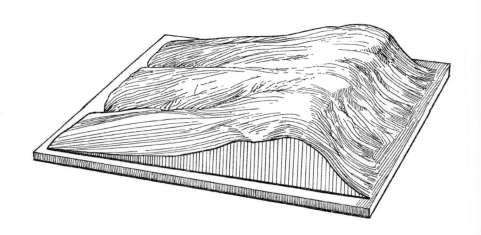

relief model

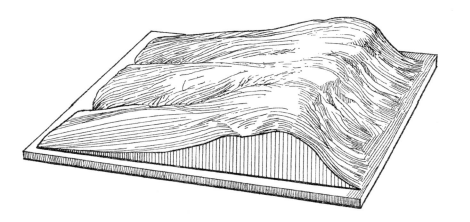

relief model

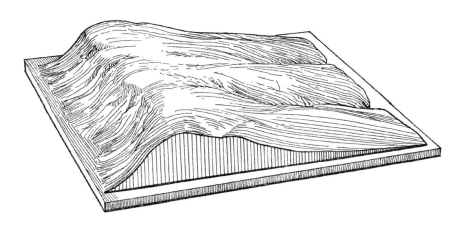

drawing of a

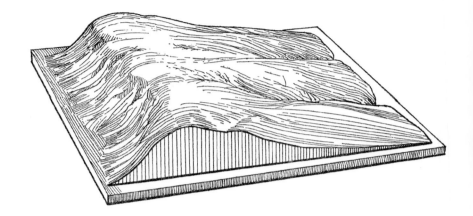

of a section

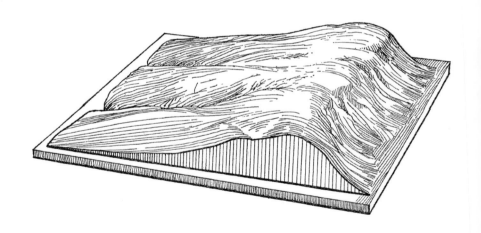

printed line

Fold

Folded

Folded

Fold

....

Geeooggrraapphhy

"It is obvious that in printing from a relief block those portions of the face of the block which come in contact with the paper will produce corresponding solid marks on the paper, whether they be lines, dots, or larger portions of the surface."

—*The Printed Book*, Harry G. Aldis, Cambridge 1916.

p.41–47: Overprintings of four maps from *London's Country, By Road, Stream and Fieldpath, Guide No.2, South of the Thames*. London, c.1923: Abinger, Gomshall, Wotton; Albury, Merrow Downs, Shere; Banstead Heath, Betchworth, Reigate; Dorking, Leith Hill, Ranmore.

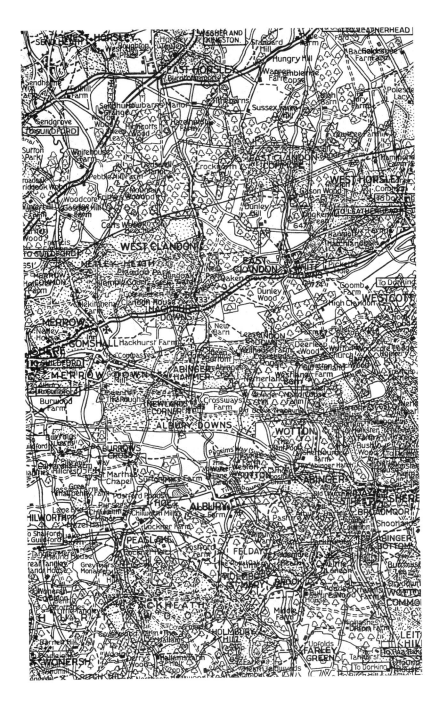

1. Abinger, Albury, Gomshall, Merrow Downs, Shere, Wotton.

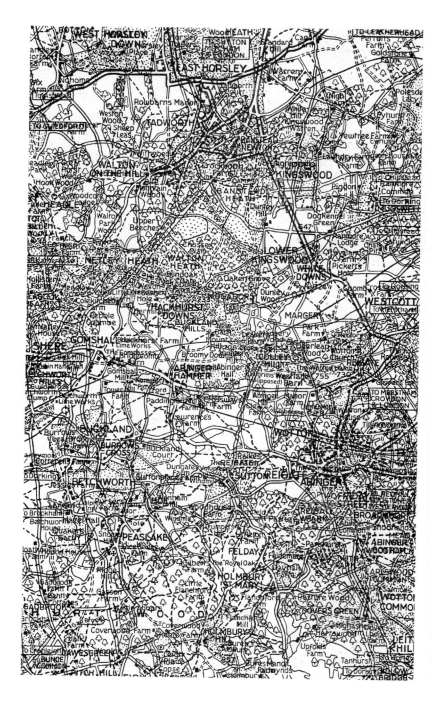

2. Abinger, Banstead Heath, Betchworth, Gomshall, Reigate, Wotton.

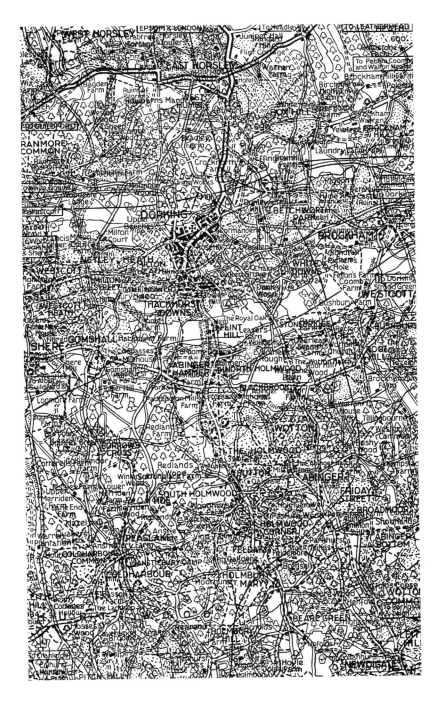

3. Abinger, Dorking, Gomshall, Leith Hill, Ranmore, Wotton.

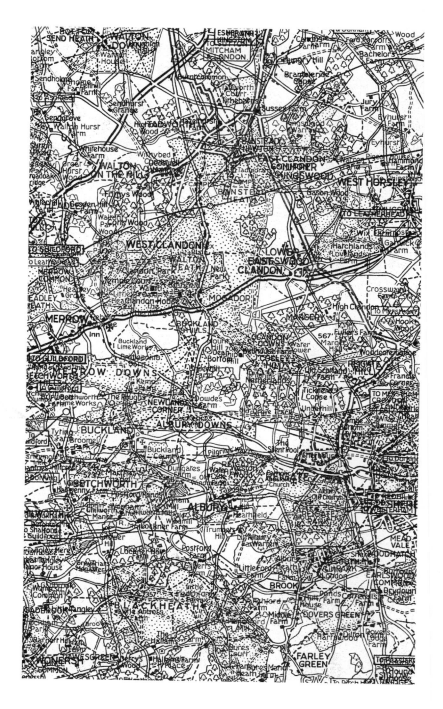

4. Albury, Banstead Heath, Betchworth, Merrow Downs, Reigate, Shere.

5. Albury, Dorking, Leith Hill, Merrow Downs, Ranmore, Shere.

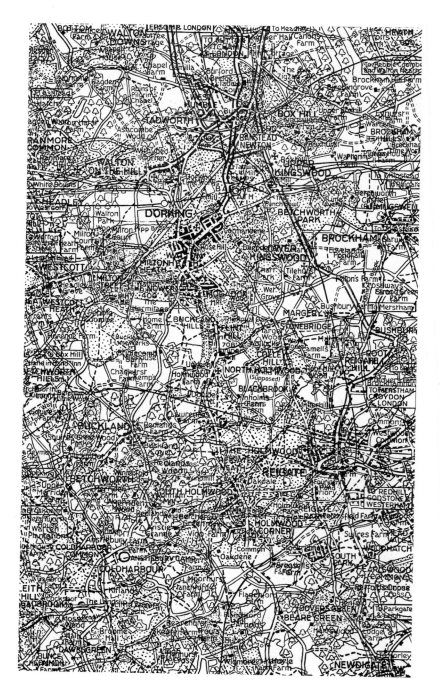

6. Banstead Heath, Betchworth, Dorking, Leith Hill, Ranmore, Reigate

46

7. Abinger, Albury, Banstead Heath, Betchworth, Dorking, Gomshall, Leith Hill, Merrow Downs, Ranmore, Reigate, Shere, Wotton.

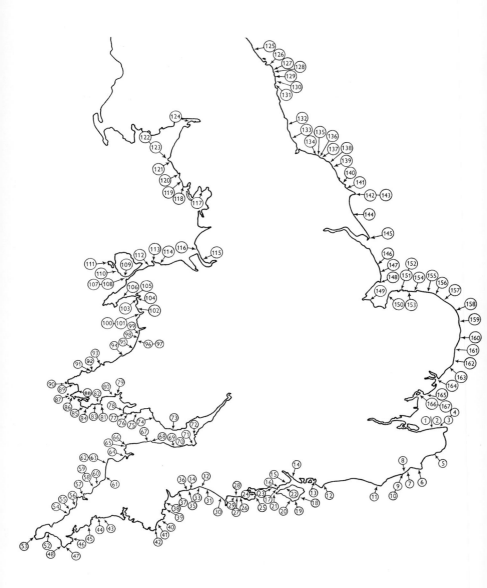

Hereabouts

"...to Land's End, up the Bristol Channel to near Cardiff, and then along the coast of South Wales to the far end of the Tenby peninsular. The route then follows the Pembrokeshire coast, Cardigan Bay, and the Lleyn Peninsular to the Menai Strait. A brief reconnaissance of Anglesey precedes the continuation along the coast of North Wales, Lancashire, and Cumberland to the Solway Firth. The journey recommences at Berwick and follows the east coast as far as the Thames... from London via the Channel coast..."

—After 'Notes on the Plates' in *The Coast of England and Wales in Pictures*, J. A. Steers, Cambridge 1960.

axe by deflected mouth of seaton shingle slightly spit ... at bay beer chalk cliffs head seaton ... at beer chalk cliffs devon foundered hooken landslip masses of south under ... bay ladram near showing sidmouth stacks ... almost at bar blocking estuary sand teign teignmouth ... and arch caves corbyn cut head in natural permian rocks torquay ... and cliffs composed dart devonian drowned estuary mudstones of slates valley ... bee sands ... point start ... bay cornwall lantivet south ... drowned estuary fowey inland of over polruan river ... dodman the ... and beach black cherts cove deposits eroded gravelly head in killas nellys obliquely of on platform porthallow raised resting rock sandy series slates stratified veryan ... also basse bay beach blown enys formed forms from head horneblende hot in is kennack lizard made of platform point reefs sand schist serpentine storm which with ... along and cove cut detail due erosion faults in is its kynance partly rocks serpentine to ... mount stmichaels ... castellated character emphatic end granite is lands of ... beach perran ... coastline devonian head in indented kelsey newquay slates west ... bay cliffs cliff-top devonian fort head in iron-age slates trevelgue watergate ... camel composed country devonian estuary harbour here of padstow rock slates ... age all buildings but dark famous from head headland is mainland of on scattered separated settlement this tintagel which ... at cut devonian gorge hanging in is mouth of phyllites rocky tintagel upper valley ... along back boscastle cut harbour has into joints land sea ... active bude coast composed cornish culm dipping erosion here in measures north of on progress south steeply ... anticline are basset begins cliffs composed consist culm dips edges hartland limb measures milford mill mouth near of other pinnacle quay sandstone second shore-reefs spekes that towards water where ... along and at culm down fall flowing foot in is limb milford mill mouth of sandstones sharp spekes stream strike syncline water waterfall ... ho pebble ridge westward ... baggy bay forms headland morte point sands that woolacombe ... and bull coast forms hardly in is it jagged morte of point promontory really reefs right-angled shows slates true turn ... almost and at bounded by castle coast end grits hard is it lynton now of parallel road rock rocks rugged runs shales streamless valley wall weathered where with ... at coast composed devon devonian dipping foreland here north of point rocks steeply ... anchor and anticline are at axis beds been being blue by capped cliffs collapse due erosion folded formed have headland horizontal into is lias mainly marine of point produced profile rhaetic rocks shallow somerset to trias undercutting vertical ... at bay bridgwater by coast ledges lias low lower of out picked rock seaweed tide ... island low mud-flats steart tide … bay brean carboniferous down limestone of outlier weston … and breaksea clays coast form lias limestone lower of point … burrows dunes kenfig sand steel works … bay beaches gower peninsular pwll-du storm … along carboniferous cliffs coast cut gower head in limestone peninsular south to well-bedded worms … and are beds carboniferous carved cliffs coast foxhole gower highly in inclined limestone of peninsular plateau port-eynon slade south-east … backed bay by drift dunes glacial gower hills of old peninsular red rhossili sand sandstone terrace … estuary of point river taf wharley … cliffs coastal cut date foreland fronting geological in line of old recent red sandstone sea … caldy erosion island marine of plain well-developed … age bedded cliffs grit in lydstep millstone of point sandstone vertically … bay beds coastline eroded is lie manorbier nearly of old out red sandstone that vertical … along been bosherston by eroded fault gash has huntsmans leap pembrokeshire sea vertical-fault … and arch are bridge carboniferous caves cut green head in limestone of pembrokeshire plateau saddle wales … at bay end gateholm island marloes of west … island isle midland ordovician point rocks skomer volcanic wooltack … broad coal haven in measures monocline pembrokeshire sandstone sleek stone … at cambrian coast cut drowned interior middle nature of pembrokeshire plateau rocks scenery solva through valley … and carn erosional ffald head island llidi of outliers ramsey stdavids to … cliffs gwaelod in llandovery mudstones pwll … at bay coast cwm eglwys newport pembrokeshire yr … cemmaes cliffs coastal folding head in mudstones of ordovician south … aberayron bay cardigan coast new quay of … coastal foreshore fronting llanrhystyd narrow near plain … aberystwyth and at mouths of rheidol ystwyth … aberystwyth alternations consist cormorant cut evenly-bedded grits hereabouts in near of on platform regular rock sea shales shore stack which … aberystwyth bay by cardigan clarach deflected drowned is misfit near of one running shingle-bar smaller stream this to valleys … aberystwyth bedding coastal cliffs in mudstones north of planes silurian well-developed with … barmouth bay enclosing estuary mawddach ro sand-spit wen … at estuary low mawddach tide … dome dyffryn fringe harlech morfa mountains of sand-dunes west … and harlech morfa mountains snowdonian … creek on marshes talsarnau … castle criccieth … at hooked llanbedrog pwllheli sand-spit trwyn … aber at menai newborough point sand-spit warren … dinorwic menai port strait … anglesey boulder-clay church islet llangwyfan of on … anglesey at bay bays beaches coast complex composed heads here mona of on rocks sandy short small tre-arddur west … are cliffs hereabouts highest holyhead in islands

south stack two ... allt and coastal composed conway low-lying
mountain of ordovician rocks strip to volcanic wen ... almost
carboniferous cliffs horizontally-bedded in limestone ... and bay
colwyn great head little orme penmaen tan ... are beach bunter cliffs
dingle facing liverpool low marine-eroded mersey mottled of point
sandstone south upper ... along alt and blundellsands by changed
characteristic coast course erosion expanse flowing foreshore
formally frequently its led of river sand serious shore this to wide ...
and carboniferous composed escarpment estuary fault head is leven
limestone of park rocks silurian topography ... above and are below
between boulder-clay clay cliffs foreshore glacial gravel gutterby hill
laminated loamy mainly material miles north of on probably rest
sand silecroft spa summer they two with ... annaside banks boulder-
clay cliffs erosion in of ... and are at by deflected details drigg esk
eskmeals estuary evolution form in irt its mite north obscure of part
point sands sand-spit single south to ... and are beach beck beneath
boulder-clay by capped cliffs course distant formed glacial gravels
hill is isolated mid-glacial now of old on reaches resting rottington
sands sandstone sea scar small stbees storm through turns
westward ... boulders coast form head large of one scars stbees this
... age cliffs in of sandstone stbees triassic well-bedded ... and beach
between boulder-clay bowness bridge by foreshore marine narrow of
raised road solway strip warp with ... forshore greens group haven
in limestone middle of strata syncline ... bamburgh castle dunes
knoll on rocky sand stands surround that which ... and beadnell
behind dyke foreshore harbour limestone north of sandbanks
sandstone underlying whin white ... bay beadnell dunes ... and
castle craster dip dunstanburgh harbour of scarp sill slopes small
whin ... and columnar contorted cullernose limestone point whin
... alnmouth at bay end far harbour of to warkworth ... bedded
caves holey limestones permian rock roker upper thin with ...
bedded black caves hall limestones permian rocks with ... bedded
black brecciated dolomites hall in limestones on permian reef rocks
same stack succession ... at base boulby boulder- clay cliffs lias lower
middle nab show staithes ... and cliffs fine lias north staithes thereof
... alum and beck bed beds cliff dogger eller estuarine foreshore
forms highest is jet lias mulgrave near of part port rock shales top
upper with ... bay runswick ... alum and are at bay beds black cliff
cliffs dogger estuarine exposed floor foot forming is jet lias lowest
nab of old only opposite outlying platform rock saltwick sandstone
shale stacks tides upper works ... and backed bay boulder-clay by
cliffs enclosed fine fylingdales give hood's ledges lias lofty moor
north of place robin south steep sweeps to which within ... and at

beds cliffs cornbrash clay corallian dipping gently in nab oxford yons
... bay filey ... flamborough head ... blow-hole boulder-clay chalk
covered flamborough formed head is of with ... active boulder-clay
cliffs coast erosion grimston holderness in of ... head spurn ...
eroded forshore lincolnshire near sutton ... and beach coast cusps
dunes lincolnshire ... gibraltar point ridges sand skegness ... at
holbeach low mud-flats outfall stmatthew tide welland ... at base
bed carstone chalk cliffs greensand hunstanton lower red sponge
white ... head island scolt ... and head island laterals marsh salt
scolt shingle ... and holkham marshes natural reclaimed wells-next-
the-sea woods ... blakeney church marshes morston ... and are cliffs
common fallen glacial gradually material materials of removes sea
sherringham slips ... boulder-clay cliffs coast in norfolk on
overstrand ... bacton by cliffs erosion exposed medieval of wall ...
sand-dunes winterton ... by deflected great is mouth of spit yare
yarmouth ... beach benacre broad by dammed sea ... beach
minsmere ... alde at ness orford river slaughden ... haven ness
orford ... clay estuary foreshore freston hall london on orwell ...
and colne marshes point salt sand spit ... mersea west ... creek low
mud-flats ray ridge sand tide ... at coast kent north reculver ...
and are by church defences erosion is preserved reculver sea severe
strong towers ... and at bay birchington chalk cliffs erosion exposed
foreshore gently low of sloping tide ... birchington chalk cliffs ...
and at chalk cliffs in folkestone landslips steep warren ... by
dungeness growth picked of out ridges shingle vegetation ... alluvial
and ashdown former gate marsh meadow of sand sea-cliff strand
winchelsea ... abandoned along altered and coast guards level much
near new now pett sea-cliff sea-wall station ... and ashdown clay
cliffs fairlight formed glen hastings of sand south-east ... ashdown
below cliffs cut ecclesbourne glen hastings in is ravine sand ...
birling chalk cliffs gap near seven sisters ... as estuary harbour
impounding known pagham sandspits shallow ... channel chichester
... at estuary hamble low tide ... beaulieu estuary in marsh of river
salt spartina ... at keyhaven marshes salt ... and at castle hurst
keyhaven marshes salt spit ... barton bay christchurch eastern of
part sands ... beds country dune harbour heath of on poole sandy
side south studland tertiary ... and chalk cliffs foreland in point
stacks vertical ... coast dorset eastwards from lulworth ... cove east
forest fossil lulworth of ... and coast cove dorset lulworth of to west
... chalk cliffs coast door dorset durdle from west ... beach chesil ...
and bridport cliff inferior of oolite sands ... bay cap golden lyme ...
and black coastal forward gault greensand landslips lias lower over
sliding ven

Illus.

Two hundred years ago Thomas Bewick made compositions out of boxwood and ink, and what they show is a proposal of a place, often a creature or person, or sometimes an event. The centre of the vignette is the subject, and the focus—all coming together and unfolding, connected by paper and impression. What is depicted is both idealised and ordinary, not just typical, but particular, and showing at its edges is the sky, and the ground, or rather their absence; the world around and beyond imagined forever.

Illus.

Stonehenge, named and framed; and all about, the view, its land-scape as it were. The miscellany of stones, behind the wire-fence, the flat grey sky and the wooded distance; all neatly titled inside the ruled edge. Post the card, by way of a communication, its rigid stock, from here to there, and not show where it sits but just its look. Or take it back, and prop or put away as a record, a reminder of the event, inadequate and partial of course—anywhere only ever as much what can be seen from it as how it might appear.

STONEHENGE, NEAR SALISBURY.

3689

Illus.

Transcribed in black line, Geoffrey Hutchings' landscapes are more or less invisible, the definition their substance, blank paper above and below both sky and incline. Their purpose was as figures, by way of example, means in the process of being able to look and interpret, and to draw and understand. Although they are views that have largely remain unaltered, at least from distance, the prevailing time seems passed, when an inked line would show a place, and we could know it, both by recognition and by its annotation.

ESCARPMENT OF THE HYTHE BEDS | ESCARPMENT OF THE CHALK

Leith Hill
Tilburstow Hill
Beechwood Hill (Tandridge)
Box Hill
Reigate Hill
Gravelly Hill (Caterham)

Obsequent valley of Gibbs Brook
Pollards Wood Lane
Obsequent valley of the Oxted Stream
Merstham Gap

Illus.

The field-by-field classification and mapping of the entire country undertaken by the Land Utilisation Survey during the 1930s was summarised and evaluated in the five-hundred pages of *The Land of Britain: Its Use and Misuse* by L. Dudley Stamp, published in 1947. The numerous illustrations—maps, charts, diagrams—include just three photographs: an abandoned Welsh hill farm; examples of wind-distorted trees in Cornwall; and this wintry landscape of water meadows on the river Itchen in Hampshire.

Illus.

A small page of John Constable's countryside, from his sketchbook
of 1813, by offset litho on handmade stock, published in facsimile
by Her Majesty's Stationery Office for the V&A Museum in 1973. The
painter's personal book, its pencilled and smudged grades of skies
and hedges and woods, record in particular that seen 'in the field', on
this day and at this time. A plain pocket aide-mémoire, made multiple
a century and a half later, away and beyond its modest intention, to
elsewhere, his own hand now passing on unbeknown.

Located

"Wreyland is land by the Wrey, a little stream in Devonshire. The Wrey flows into the Bovey, and the Bovey into the Teign, and the Teign flows into the sea at Teignmouth. The land is on the east side of the Wrey, just opposite the village of Lustleigh. It forms a manor, and gives its name to a hamlet of six houses, of which this is one."

—Cecil Torr's careful pinpointing of place, from the preface to his *Small Talk at Wreyland*, Cambridge 1918.

Mapped

Equal names and numbers, shapes and lines, nowhere undefined by boundary or by words. Every single place a centre, while edges are cut off abrupt and non-transitional—what extends, extends from. The lineated roads and winding streams and paths, the blank or infilled demarcations, all of a piece; jigsawed and finished for the present.

Notes

[ ]
A roll of paper tape gummed solid after being stored in a damp workshop.

Aggregate
Published as a casebound edition reproducing each of the hundred squares, or layers, page by page (1994). Originally included in *Wirelesslessness* (1992), and in *Distance etc.* (1999), *Englshpublshing* (2004), and *Uniformagazine* no.6 (2016).

Bbbn
Published as *BBBN*, a four-page letterpress pamphlet, 1998; also included in *Distance etc.* (1999) and *essayes* (2001).

Collection
First published as *Bunch*, colour facsimiles of thirty labels, printed inkjet and casebound, 2005. The texts included in *Distance etc.* (1999) and *Englshpublshing* (2004), while the commentary was written for the entry 'Collection' in *Anticipatory history* (2011).

Directory
The first printing of the locational map; the text and the sequence of phone numbers initially published as 'Exchange', in *Distance etc.* (1999) and *Englshpublshing* (2004), where they are illustrated by two examples from a set of record cards of locational details.

Escarpment
Published as a twelve-page digital pamphlet, 2010.

Hereabouts
Published as *about*, a sixteen-page digital pamphlet, 2009; included earlier in *Distance etc.* (1999), *Englshpublshing* (2004), and *Uniformagazine* no.7 (2016).

Located
Included in *Specimens* (1998), *Distance etc.* (1999), *Englshpublshing* (2004), and *Uniformagazine* no.9 (2017).

Notes
Notes to the parts, the centre notes: its references and commentaries. *Printed landscape* has been selected from a miscellany of work published since the early 1990s, reformatted and arranged alphabetically. The subjects are commonly about *geography*, its interpretation and abstraction on the printed page. The locations are often places of familiarity and association, from across southern England, while the book has to do with making connections between its modalities. As with places, or *types* of places—its subject as such—the reading is intendedly multi-directional.

Ringinging
Published in *Englshpublshing* (2004), and as an eight-page digital pamphlet, 2007.

Some
A version was published as *some form*, a thirty-two page letterpress 'reverse-reading' pamphlet, 1995; also included in *rereader* (1996), and in *Englshpublshing* (2004), and *Wordage* (2011).

Ticket
A version of this text was published as a sixteen-page digital pamphlet, 2012. As a teenager I regularly took a bus journey directly south through the suburbs and beyond (see frontispiece photo), arriving at the final stop on the route where I would walk a few miles in the country at the edge of the downs—a wad of return tickets collated in my pocket.

Union
Les Coleman's booklet *Glue* (In House Publishing 2002) is a sequence of blank pages each affixed to the next with a different adhesive. The list of Contents reads: Coccoina, Copydex, Gloy, Multi-Purpose Water Glue, Ocacell Cellulose Adhesive, Pickup, Platignum Studio Gum, Pritt, PVA, Spray Mount, Stephens Golden Gum, and UHU.

Vignettes
Published as *Spate*, a sixteen-page digital pamphlet, 2009. The quotation is cited in *Landscape and Western Art*, Malcom Andrews, Oxford 1999.

Walk
Flyposters, Axminster, 5th January 2012; the photographs were taken by Bethan Sackett-Thomas for inclusion in *Forth & Back*, a project by Tamsin Clark. "…an invitation to design a poster, post it somewhere and document the piece in its chosen location. The poster can rest as a temporarily situated object, an announcement, or simply as a gesture put forth…" Also printed in *Uniformagazine* no.2 (2015).

X
"The way into the Axe book is by way of what it is not. From the front of the book the right-hand page sequence follows the direction of the river from sea to source, from the back the left-hand sequence moves downstream with the river's flow. This self-cancelling movement is cut across at forty-one points by bridges of different kinds. Books have beginnings and ends, front and back covers, but the linear movement is replaced here by a transverse one, raising questions about where, when and why each of the crossings took place. The illustrations at the same time forgo the bridges themselves, picturesque or piquant as many of them are. This is not a sequence of calendar portraits: the crossings are present only as points of vantage, looking up or downstream… The book interrupts the conventional river story-line of rise, accumulation and outflow, refuses to be sidetracked by the celebratory spirit, and redirects attention onto the human imperatives that have intersected a natural conduit at different times and for different reasons. It offers neither comfort nor manifesto; it is about landscape, settlement and communication: necessary engagements with a natural feature that remains unchanged. It shows a way of looking at the Axe valley as it has evolved in collaboration with man: not so much nature writing as human geography."
—*Rare Sighting in the Haldon Hills*, J. C. C. Mays, CCANW, Exeter 2009.

Years etc.
Written for a leaflet to accompany an exhibition of publications by Richard Long; also included in *Distance etc.* (1999).

Other parts previously unprinted.

Selected bibliography
—*Wirelesslessness*, Coracle 1992.
—*Aggregate*, 1994.
—*some form*, 1995.
—*rereader: selected reading and writing ninetyone to ninetysix*, 1996.
—*BBBN*, 1998.
—*Specimens*, 1998.
—*Distance etc.: Longereadingandwriting ninetyfourtoninetynine*, 1999.
—*Numeracy, uniformity and structure: three publications of the work of Richard Long*, Dundee Contemporary Arts 1999.
—*essayes*, 2001.
—*Englshpublshing: Writing and readings 1991–2002*, Coracle, Spacex, Sixtus 2004.
—*Bunch*, 2005.
—*The True Line: The Landscape Diagrams of Geoffrey Hutchings*, 2006.
—*Ringinging*, 2007.
—*River Axe Crossings: A visual survey along the course of the river*, 2008.
—*about*, 2009.
—*Geeooggrraapphhy*, 2009.
—*Spate: Flooded Landscape near Exeter*, 2009.
—*escarpment*, 2010.
—*Anticipatory history* ed. DeSilvey, Naylor, Sackett, Uniformbooks 2011.
—*Wordage*, Uniformbooks 2011.
—*'ticket'*, 2012.
—*Uniformagazine* nos.1–10, 2014–17.
(Self-published unless stated.)

There are also online versions of many of these works: Writings and readings, index: colin sackett.co.uk/writing_readings_26.php

names and numbers as much as shapes and lines names and numbers
as much as shapes and lines names and numbers as much as shapes
and lines names and numbers as much as shapes and lines names and
numbers as much as shapes and lines names and numbers as much
as shapes and lines names and numbers as much as shapes and lines
names and numbers as much as shapes and lines names and numbers
as much as shapes and lines names and numbers as much as shapes
and lines names and numbers as much as shapes and lines names and
numbers as much as shapes and lines names and numbers as much
as shapes and lines names and numbers as much as shapes and lines
names and numbers as much as shapes and lines names and numbers
as much as shapes and lines names and numbers as much as shapes
and lines names and numbers as much as shapes and lines names and
numbers as much as shapes and lines names and numbers as much
as shapes and lines names and numbers as much as shapes and lines
names and numbers as much as shapes and lines names and numbers
as much as shapes and lines names and numbers as much as shapes
and lines names and numbers as much as shapes and lines names and
numbers as much as shapes and lines names and numbers as much
as shapes and lines names and numbers as much as shapes and lines
names and numbers as much as shapes and lines names and numbers
as much as shapes and lines names and numbers as much as shapes
and lines names and numbers as much as shapes and lines names and
numbers as much as shapes and lines names and numbers as much
as shapes and lines names and numbers as much as shapes and lines
names and numbers as much as shapes and lines names and numbers
as much as shapes and lines names and numbers as much as shapes
and lines names and numbers as much as shapes and lines names and
numbers as much as shapes and lines names and numbers as much
as shapes and lines names and numbers as much as shapes and lines
names and numbers as much as shapes and lines names and numbers
as much as shapes and lines names and numbers as much as shapes
and lines names and numbers as much as shapes and lines names and
numbers as much as shapes and lines names and numbers as much
as shapes and lines names and numbers as much as shapes and lines
names and numbers as much as shapes and lines names and numbers
as much as shapes and lines names and numbers as much as shapes
and lines names and numbers as much as shapes and lines names and
numbers as much as shapes and lines names and numbers as much
as shapes and lines names and numbers as much as shapes and lines

shapes and lines as much as names and numbers shapes and lines as much as names and numbers

Printing

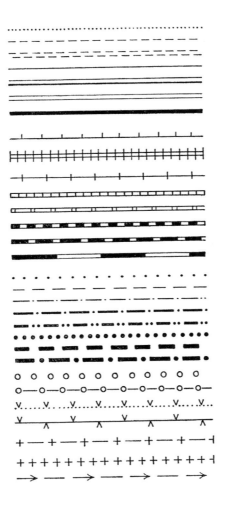

'Varieties of Line' from *Maps and Diagrams: their compilation and construction*,
F. J. Monkhouse and H. R. Wilkinson, London & New York, 1952.

Ringinging

The phone number of Leith Hill tower is 01306 712434—its viewing platform, at exactly 1000–feet, is the highest point in south-eastern England.

'View of Leith Hill. From a sketch taken during the Government Survey in 1844' (detail) from *History of Surrey*, E. W. Brayley, London 1878.

Some

Succession is the intrinsic development whereby communities of increasing bulk and complexity occupy the site in gradual sequence tending towards the ultimate establishment of a more or less stable community known as the climax which is dominated by the largest and particularly the tallest and when these become dominant the climax is some form of woodland some form of woodland some form of woodland some form of woodland some form of woodland some form of woodland some form of woodland some form of woodland some form of woodland some form of woodland some form of woodland some form of woodland some form of woodland some form of woodland some form of woodland some form of woodland some form of woodland some form of woodland some form of woodlan some form of woodla some form of woodl some form of wood some form of woo some form of wo some form of w some form of some form o some form some for some fo some f some som so s

—After the entries 'Climax' and 'Succession' in the glossary to *London's Countryside: Geographical field work for students and teachers of geography*, S. W. Wooldridge & Geoffrey E. Hutchings, London 1957.

'The North Downs near Reigate' (Aerofilms Ltd).

Ticket

t'icket	t'icket	t'icket	t'icket	t'icket	t'icket
ti'cket	ti'cket	ti'cket	ti'cket	ti'cket	ti'cket
tic'ket	tic'ket	tic'ket	tic'ket	tic'ket	tic'ket
tick'et	tick'et	tick'et	tick'et	tick'et	tick'et
ticke't	ticke't	ticke't	ticke't	ticke't	ticke't
tick'et	tick'et	tick'et	tick'et	tick'et	tick'et
tic'ket	tic'ket	tic'ket	tic'ket	tic'ket	tic'ket
ti'cket	ti'cket	ti'cket	ti'cket	ti'cket	ti'cket
t'icket	t'icket	t'icket	t'icket	t'icket	t'icket
ti'cket	ti'cket	ti'cket	ti'cket	ti'cket	ti'cket
tic'ket	tic'ket	tic'ket	tic'ket	tic'ket	tic'ket
tick'et	tick'et	tick'et	tick'et	tick'et	tick'et
ticke't	ticke't	ticke't	ticke't	ticke't	ticke't
tick'et	tick'et	tick'et	tick'et	tick'et	tick'et
tic'ket	tic'ket	tic'ket	tic'ket	tic'ket	tic'ket
ti'cket	ti'cket	ti'cket	ti'cket	ti'cket	ti'cket
t'icket	t'icket	t'icket	t'icket	t'icket	t'icket
ti'cket	ti'cket	ti'cket	ti'cket	ti'cket	ti'cket
tic'ket	tic'ket	tic'ket	tic'ket	tic'ket	tic'ket
tick'et	tick'et	tick'et	tick'et	tick'et	tick'et
ticke't	ticke't	ticke't	ticke't	ticke't	ticke't
tick'et	tick'et	tick'et	tick'et	tick'et	tick'et
tic'ket	tic'ket	tic'ket	tic'ket	tic'ket	tic'ket
ti'cket	ti'cket	ti'cket	ti'cket	ti'cket	ti'cket
t'icket	t'icket	t'icket	t'icket	t'icket	t'icket
ti'cket	ti'cket	ti'cket	ti'cket	ti'cket	ti'cket
tic'ket	tic'ket	tic'ket	tic'ket	tic'ket	tic'ket
tick'et	tick'et	tick'et	tick'et	tick'et	tick'et
ticke't	ticke't	ticke't	ticke't	ticke't	ticke't
tick'et	tick'et	tick'et	tick'et	tick'et	tick'et
tic'ket	tic'ket	tic'ket	tic'ket	tic'ket	tic'ket
ti'cket	ti'cket	ti'cket	ti'cket	ti'cket	ti'cket
t'icket	t'icket	t'icket	t'icket	t'icket	t'icket
ti'cket	ti'cket	ti'cket	ti'cket	ti'cket	ti'cket
tic'ket	tic'ket	tic'ket	tic'ket	tic'ket	tic'ket
tick'et	tick'et	tick'et	tick'et	tick'et	tick'et
ticke't	ticke't	ticke't	ticke't	ticke't	ticke't
tick'et	tick'et	tick'et	tick'et	tick'et	tick'et
tic'ket	tic'ket	tic'ket	tic'ket	tic'ket	tic'ket
ti'cket	ti'cket	ti'cket	ti'cket	ti'cket	ti'cket

t'icket	tick'et	tic'ket	ti'cket	ticke't	ti'cket
ti'cket	ticke't	ti'cket	tic'ket	tick'et	t'icket
tic'ket	tick'et	t'icket	tick'et	tic'ket	ti'cket
tick'et	tic'ket	ti'cket	ticke't	ti'cket	tic'ket
ticke't	ti'cket	tic'ket	tick'et	t'icket	tick'et
tick'et	t'icket	tick'et	tic'ket	ti'cket	ticke't
tic'ket	ti'cket	ticke't	ti'cket	tic'ket	tick'et
ti'cket	tic'ket	tick'et	t'icket	tick'et	tic'ket
t'icket	tick'et	tic'ket	ti'cket	ticke't	ti'cket
ti'cket	ticke't	ti'cket	tic'ket	tick'et	t'icket
tic'ket	tick'et	t'icket	tick'et	tic'ket	ti'cket
tick'et	tic'ket	ti'cket	ticke't	ti'cket	tic'ket
ticke't	ti'cket	tic'ket	tick'et	t'icket	tick'et
tick'et	t'icket	tick'et	tic'ket	ti'cket	ticke't
tic'ket	ti'cket	ticke't	ti'cket	tic'ket	tick'et
ti'cket	tic'ket	tick'et	t'icket	tick'et	tic'ket
t'icket	tick'et	tic'ket	ti'cket	ticke't	ti'cket
ti'cket	ticke't	ti'cket	tic'ket	tick'et	t'icket
tic'ket	tick'et	t'icket	tick'et	tic'ket	ti'cket
tick'et	tic'ket	ti'cket	ticke't	ti'cket	tic'ket
ticke't	ti'cket	tic'ket	tick'et	t'icket	tick'et
tick'et	t'icket	tick'et	tic'ket	ti'cket	ticke't
tic'ket	ti'cket	ticke't	ti'cket	tic'ket	tick'et
ti'cket	tic'ket	tick'et	t'icket	tick'et	tic'ket
t'icket	tick'et	tic'ket	ti'cket	ticke't	ti'cket
ti'cket	ticke't	ti'cket	tic'ket	tick'et	t'icket
tic'ket	tick'et	t'icket	tick'et	tic'ket	ti'cket
tick'et	tic'ket	ti'cket	ticke't	ti'cket	tic'ket
ticke't	ti'cket	tic'ket	tick'et	t'icket	tick'et
tick'et	t'icket	tick'et	tic'ket	ti'cket	ticke't
tic'ket	ti'cket	ticke't	ti'cket	tic'ket	tick'et
ti'cket	tic'ket	tick'et	t'icket	tick'et	tic'ket
t'icket	tick'et	tic'ket	ti'cket	ticke't	ti'cket
ti'cket	ticke't	ti'cket	tic'ket	tick'et	t'icket
tic'ket	tick'et	t'icket	tick'et	tic'ket	ti'cket

PLATE 13

A sunken lane in East Devon: Armourwood Lane, near Thorverton. It originated as a
boundary (probably in the seventh century) between the royal estate of Silverton (left)
and the Exeter Abbey estate (right). A double ditch was dug out by slave-labour, and
the earth thrown up to form hedgebanks on each side. The "two-fold ditch" thus becomes
a sunken lane running as far as the Saxon boundary required.

p.56, *The Making of the English Landscape*, W. G. Hoskins, London 1955.

PLATE 13

A sunken lane in East Devon: Armourwood Lane, near Thorverton. It originated as a
boundary (probably in the seventh century) between the royal estate of Silverton (left)
and the Exeter Abbey estate (right). A double ditch was dug out by slave-labour, and
the earth thrown up to form hedgebanks on each side. The "two-fold ditch," thus becomes
a sunken lane running as far as the Saxon boundary required.

Vignettes

"In this drawing, as in the entire tradition of panoramic landscapes that follow, surface and extent are emphasised at the expense of volume and solidity."

—Svetlana Alpers on 'Dune Landscape near Haarlem' by Hendrick Goltzius, 1603; 'The Mapping Impulse in Dutch Art', in *The Art of Describing: Dutch Art in the Seventeenth Century*, London 1983.

[p.81–86]: 'Flooded Landscape near Exeter', 2009.

Fields

Trees

Trees

Field

Trees

Field

Field

Field

Hedge

Trees

Hedge

Trees

Trees

Hedge

Tree

Hedge

Field

Hedge

Field

Hedge

Trees

Trees

Floodwater

Floodwater

Railway Track

Trees

Embankment

Field

Floodwater

Floodwater

Tree

Submerged Fence

Field

Fields   Fields

Field   Field   Field
                   Farm buildings   House
Trees   House

                              Field
                                        House   House
          Trees
                              Farmhouse

     Field
          Field   Tree   Trees

Trees   Field

          Floodwater   Floodwater
Floodwater   Tree
Railway Track   Embankment   Railway Track   Embankment

     Floodwater   Floodwater
                         Submerged Fence

Field   Field

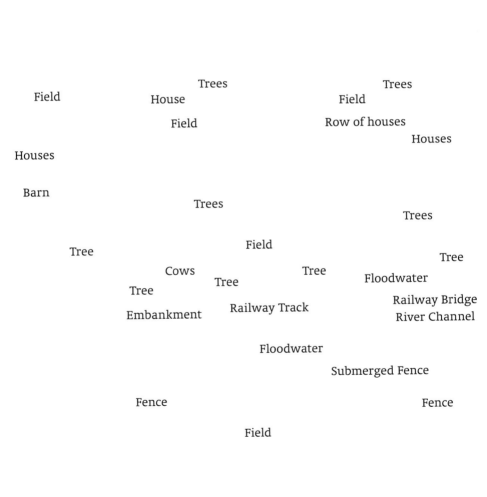

Field

Trees

House

Trees

Field

Field

Row of houses

Houses

Houses

Barn

Trees

Tree

Trees

Field

Tree

Cows

Tree

Tree

Floodwater

Tree

Railway Bridge

Embankment

Railway Track

River Channel

Floodwater

Submerged Fence

Fence

Fence

Field

Field

Trees

Fields

Houses

Trees

Houses

Trees

Trees

Trees

Trees

Floodwater

Floodwater

Floodwater

Tree

Footbridge

Trees

Trees

Trees

Railway Embankment

Floodwater

Hedge

Hedge

Field

Fence

Hedge

Hedge

Fields   Fields

Church
Houses

Trees   Trees

Footbridge

Floodwater   Trees   Floodwater

Floodwater   Trees

Railway Embankment

Field

Field

Hedge

Field   Tree
                         Hedge   Field

Tree

Trees

Trees

Trees

Fields

Trees

Fields

Trees

Trees

Floodwater

Floodwater

Railway Embankment

Barn

Hedge

Trees

Bush

Walk

From the town centre take the route south from West Street to the roundabout at the bottom of the hill. Take the road marked to Kilmington and Honiton and follow the pavement on the right over the railway bridge. Just after the bridge, cross the road and descend to the field on the left by the gate and the steps down the bank. Continue across this field parallel with the wooded embankment on the left; the river Axe is on the right. Go through the gate at the far left and under the bridge.

Continue through the small wood and cross the railway line by the two gates. Follow the footpath by the car park of the carpet factory and turn left onto the road, past the builders' merchant on the left and to the top. At the road junction turn left and continue down to the roundabout from where you can return to the town centre.

THE BRIDGE WAS ALSO CAST AS A TUNNEL FOR THE FOOTPATH

THE BRIDGE WAS ALSO CAST AS A TUNNEL FOR THE FOOTPATH

THE TUNNEL WAS ALSO CAST AS A BRIDGE FOR THE RAILWAY

THE
TUNNEL
WAS ALSO
CAST AS
A BRIDGE
FOR THE
RAILWAY

Walk

From the town centre take the route south from West Street to the roundabout at the bottom of the hill. Take the road marked to Seaton and Musbury and follow the pavement on the right passing the turning to the railway station. Turn right at the brick terraced houses and continue down past the builders' merchant, then take the footpath that leads off to the right before the entrance to the carpet factory. Cross the railway line by the two gates and go through the small wood and the tunnel.

Go through the gate directly ahead and turn to cross the field parallel with the wooded embankment on the right; the river Axe is on the left. At the far end climb the bank by the steps up to the road, go through the gate and cross over. Follow the pavement across the railway bridge and down to the roundabout from where you can return to the town centre.

X

The river Axe flows through Dorset, Somerset and Devon, rising near Beaminster, flowing west then south by Axminster and joining the English Channel at Axmouth near Seaton. During its thirty-five kilometre course it is fed by various streams and by the tributary rivers Yarty and Coly. Taken during the period November 2007 to March 2008,* the photographs look directly upstream and downstream from the centre of each of all the forty-one extant crossings,** ranging variously from plain wooden beam, to stone arch, to concrete road bridge; excluded are weirs, railway bridges, and crossings by ford or stepping stones.

* / ** see p.103

p.95–103: *River Axe Crossings: A visual survey along the course of the river,* left: looking upstream, right: looking downstream.

97

* The view of the river is in its winter state, at other times during the year the definition of the channel and the view ahead is often interrupted by bankside growth and obstructed by overhanging foliage. However, one crossing (bottom, p.99) was being rebuilt during the period and an earlier pair of photographs, taken in summer 2007 are shown; as an exception, and as an example, they show the river in the pastoral lushness of high summer.

** "…for the most part, the crossings function as standpoint rather than substance, a somewhat arbitrary link in the looping visual chain (upstream, downstream, upstream, downstream) created by the survey of the river's course. There is a curious deferral at work here, which forces the reader/viewer's attention to become aware of the simple oddity of standing above moving water, a still point in a liquid landscape."
—Caitlin DeSilvey, 'River Axe Crossings', *Journal of Historical Geography* 36, 2010.

Years etc.

....

Throughout these publications, the photographs are definitive records of moments within a landscape, whether of a single geometric form made with material from the particular terrain, or a composed view of a landscape from within the duration of a journey. Where a sculptural form has been introduced into the landscape, this will occupy a central, foregrounded position within the image. The language is distilled, precise and economical, referring numerically to periods of time (hours, days) and distances (miles), or descriptively to repeated actions (walking, throwing), forms (lines, circles), materials (stone, driftwood), and locations. The uniformity of presentation highlights the variations and particularity of each combination of text and image; the singularity of each work is established by its relationship to other works.

1976—The title of this publication is *Some notes on the work of Richard Long* by Michael Compton and it was published to coincide with and accompany an exhibition in the British Pavilion at the Venice Biennale during the summer of this year. The format is A4 portrait and consists of twenty pages wire-stitched into a white cover. With the exception of the first two pages which are blank, the text and the photographic and line illustrations are printed black letterpress throughout, while the cover is printed on the front only. The cover text, essay, captions, biography and colophon are set in Times New Roman. Integrated within the essay are thirteen photographic illustrations of works and one line illustration of an appended map, along with two illustrations of exhibition announcement cards (both of which have single photographic images). Of the thirteen works, two are appended maps, eight are physical interventions made in the landscape and three are sculptures made in galleries. The landscape and gallery photographs have a bordering rule around (with the exception of the first which bleeds on four sides), while the maps and exhibition cards do not. The works are ordered, with a few exceptions, chronologically; the majority dated as being from the previous year. In contrast to the other two publications detailed here, the choice and sequence of the images is presumably determined by the essay, which they in effect illustrate.

1977—The title of this publication is *The North Woods* and it was published on the occasion of an exhibition at the Whitechapel Art Gallery from 25th January to 27th February. The format is A4 landscape and consists of sixteen pages wire-stitched into a white cover. The text and the photographic and line illustrations are printed black offset litho throughout, while the cover is printed on the front only. The cover text, captions and colophon are set in Gill Sans. There are six photographic works and one graphic work occupying right-hand pages, while the title of each work is printed opposite on the left-hand page. The photographic works have a bordering rule and outside of that a consistent white margin to the page edge. Apart from the graphic work and the final photographic work, the titles refer to the particular physical intervention made in each location: a line made of fallen saplings in Canada; a line of stones in the Himalayas; a circle of stones in Iceland and another in Ireland; and a composition of twelve radiating stone lines on the American Prairie. The graphic work shows the irregular line of a six hour run from Dartmoor in the south to Exmoor in the north, from the bottom to the top of the page; while the final work shows a view of a wood from a journey in Japan. None of the works state the year in which they were made.

1978—The title of this publication is *Rivers and Stones* and it was published by Newlyn Orion Galleries for the exhibition 'Peter Joseph, Richard Long, David Tremlett'. The format is A4 landscape and consists of sixteen pages wire-stitched into a white cover. The text and the photographic and line illustrations are printed black offset litho throughout, while the cover is printed on the front only. The cover text, captions and colophon are set in Gill Sans. There are six photographic works occupying right-hand pages, while the title and details of each work are printed opposite on the left-hand page. They each have a bordering rule and outside of that a consistent white margin to the page edge. In addition to the textual details, the first two works are appended by a graphic rendering of the route and the basis for the extent of each particular journey. Apart from the penultimate work which is from 1974, all of the works are from the year previous to the publication, and apart from one work from Ireland and one from Switzerland they are all made in England.

Appendix: Printing & publishing

The methods of making printed pages have always changed and evolved, from the impression of formed metal and thick ink, to the repelling of water and oil on a photo-sensitised surface, to the electrostatic charge of fine powder fused by direct heat.

The activity of publishing, tethered by the economies particular to each publisher, utilises these various means to produce books and pamphlets, either handing over the entire process to printers and binders, or, as is often the case with self-publishing and artists publications, carrying out parts of the process, and becoming a book manufacturer as well.

The ability and willingness to self-produce a publication is as variable as the actual content. The traditional book, printed on quality stock, sewn and case bound, is beyond the inclination of the vast majority of those primarily concerned with simply issuing content to the world at large. However, the pamphlet, idiomatic of much self-publishing of the twentieth century, is both relatively cheap and easily-achieved—mimeographed or photocopied pages, collated, folded and stapled—a very often domestic activity.

I began producing small publications in the late 1970s, printing on a table-top letterpress machine, with hand-set type, and images made with tipped-in parts, or via relief-cuts, or etched blocks. Plain and basic things, printed in runs of never more than a hundred copies, they were part of what was a teething process. The method was always distinctly restricting, and with hindsight the limitations probably played a large part in the content itself. So text was short, page size small, extent modest; in its way the means led to the ends.

With the restrictions always in mind, elaboration was by integrating other parts from elsewhere, to combine what could be done in-house with what might be brought in. Change isn't a necessity of course, the restrictive can provide opportunity to entrench and pursue endless variation; but the pursuit of hybrids wasn't the choice, this was an experiment in trying things out, to see what was possible, while at the same time looking for what might necessarily be the content and subject.

Over the next thirty years, working with, and alongside, artists, writers, printers, and publishers, differences and similarities were gradually made plain. The distinct matters of choice, and of concern. It became obvious that to publish was to have a preoccupation with the book itself: how it could be made, how it could be used, and how it could be read.

The structure of sequence, and direction, the gathering and grouping of content, became the subject of many attempts and demonstrations, in each instance informed by what had gone before. This wasn't exactly a regular list of titles, a pile of books, not an accumulation in a linear sense, but an expanding whole, the parts placed at the edge of something that gradually defined its own limits.[1]

The content was more often than not borrowed, or commandeered, for new usage. Edited piecemeal from sources such as geographical texts, modernist literature, radio transcripts, the book became a structure for fragments to be placed and read, by page, and then in the further diminishing units of line and word and letter. Not a literary project as such, but a deployment of text as a conceptual tool for the disruption of meaning and structure. There was always a subject, or a focus, also inherited from the source: a type of place; a type of sound; a type of direction, or action.

The making of a pasted-up artwork, using photosetting and drawn or processed line-work, placed, and fixed with adhesive, was the prime activity for print production prior to computer formatting. Whether for photocopy or offset litho the means was the same, and the final printed page disguised the process, only the method of reproduction, be it ink or toner, was actually evident.

Other means were available, not used or practical in a commercial sense, but nonetheless perfect for limited use. In the early 1990s I published several substantial books in batches, small, but not limited, editions. These used an electric typewriter, with black carbon and white correction ribbons, the content printed directly and individually onto coloured stock; and similarly a series of handwritten pamphlets made with a black rapidograph pen. The activity of physically typing and writing seemed historically linked to the repetitive practices of the mechanical and clerical office, or the monastic scriptorium—the processes had been moved somewhat out of their time.

Some means changed, but others remained constant, so, the hand-printing of short letterpress texts was used for a publication in 2003 as it had been twenty years earlier. Whereas pages printed with a domestic inkjet machine only began around that time, the coloured content composed and designed on-screen, compressing the process of editing and production.

I can't recall now an interim period between when a job was supplied to a printer in artwork form, to make a litho plate, via process camera and repro film, and now, when data is sent as a high-resolution pdf, and content arrives digitally on paper seemingly without further process. The direct interplay between writing, editing and constructing pages on-screen marked the most significant change in the physical making of books. The process of gathering text and manipulating the fit and extent within one device was key to the compression of what were previously separate activities into a new autonomy: the publisher could be writer, editor, designer, typesetter, and printer, all from the same desk.

When, in 2007, having avoided the idea for long enough, I decided to make a website, a simple question presented itself. Was it possible to consider what you saw within the bounds of the monitor as a sheet of paper, and so was the edge of the screen equivalent to the edge of the page? I didn't have any understanding of how to begin, but I had an idea of how I thought it should look, and how I wanted it to be structured. The coder I worked with made a template where the text and images were placed on what was equivalent to a piece of white paper.

Once we had this simple style, it was then easy to duplicate page after page and begin the role of online publisher. Works that had been made primarily as books, where the physical division of paged content emphasised structure and sequence, were now reformatted as a single page: the format as wide as the frame of the browser, and the extent of unlimited depth.

Basic HTML allowed simple variations to be applied to text; trial and error the process of learning. It was picked up as a system and it either worked correctly, or it was wrong. Pages could be published, then amended, and amended again, without the finality there is with print. During the next few years I published about thirty pages of online work.[2] New versions made in and for a browser, assembled from the raw materials of scanned or cut and pasted text, digital images, manuscripts and typescripts, to be read in the identical form that they were constructed. The entire process of publishing done within the illuminated bounds of the device, and the process of reading done likewise.

For the last several years, my focus has been on publishing a general series of determinedly physical books.[3] Models for independent publishing have changed markedly, books can now reach readers direct, via online networks of targeted information and focus. With the two modes, online publishing and printed books, the uncertainty about what publishing now is, what it has become through these parallel tools, is often characterised as undergoing some sort of uncertainty, even crisis. The prevailing tendency is to look for what is flawed: the fugitiveness of platforms and hardware, markets and exploitation, examples with tendencies towards the potentially defunct.

Hence the animated turning of pages in pdf readers such as issuu, FlippingBook, their simulation of the act; the books with what often appear to be just the symptoms of books, produced by Blurb, Lulu, and Lightning Source, effortlessly, and at will. (The nature of that will varying from caution to blind optimism, and thereby the production of the single unique example to the first batch, a handful, or a room-full.) And the comparative effort of reading the extended and the succinct, the blog or the tweet, desire and restraint as causal components for mass behavioural change, in terms of attention at least. The polarity of total availability created by ubuweb, monoskop, aaaaarg, and the commercial aggression and self-interest of Amazon, can be turned on and off at a click, the inherent moral politics as plain as day.

The vast archival load taken on voluntarily and posted online in the last decade, the attention to accurately present the nuances of printed forms, the physicality of paper and print illuminated on screen, has had effect in creating and establishing a meticulous aesthetic of the historical. The scanned or photographed vernacular document is now uploaded and classified, searched for and located, freely distributed after the event. What had once become elusive, gone out of print, scarce and hidden and thereby of its time, can be made available once more. Republished, facsimiled, itself again.

Strictly speaking, publication is always to do with exchange; either by commerce, as in the traditional production and sale of physical books, or, by making online content available to view and to take—a radically different quality and scope to the connections between publisher and reader. During its first years of activity, Uniformbooks has attempted to keep a momentum of publication, and while online platforms and social media provide formats for posting regular announcements and fresh content, the actual books appear somewhat erratically. The diversity of the titles we publish results in several arriving at once, and we go to press as soon as possible, without the planned marketing schedules of trade publishing.

Printed offset litho and launched in Autumn 2014, Uniformagazine is intended as a quarterly occurrence alongside the books,[4] for the variety of writers, artists and contributors that we work with and publish, as well as for slighter or peripheral content; not necessarily thematic, but with that possibility. As singular as the daily blog entry, as restricted as the tweet, the plain form of the pamphlet has persisted throughout the history of publishing, its flexibility and limited extent perfectly suited to a single subject or to simple gatherings of text and imagery.

1. Bibliography 1984–2016: colinsackett.co.uk/bibliography.php
2. Writings and readings, index: colin sackett.co.uk/writing_readings_26.php
3. Uniformbooks is an independent imprint for the visual and literary arts, cultural geography and history, music and bibliographic studies. The first book, Anticipatory history, was published in autumn 2011; Printed landscape is the twenty-fourth title.
4. Ten issues of Uniformagazine were published, the last dated Summer 2017.

—Originally titled 'Publishing then then publishing' and included in Code–X: Paper, Ink, Pixel and Screen, Farnham, 2015.